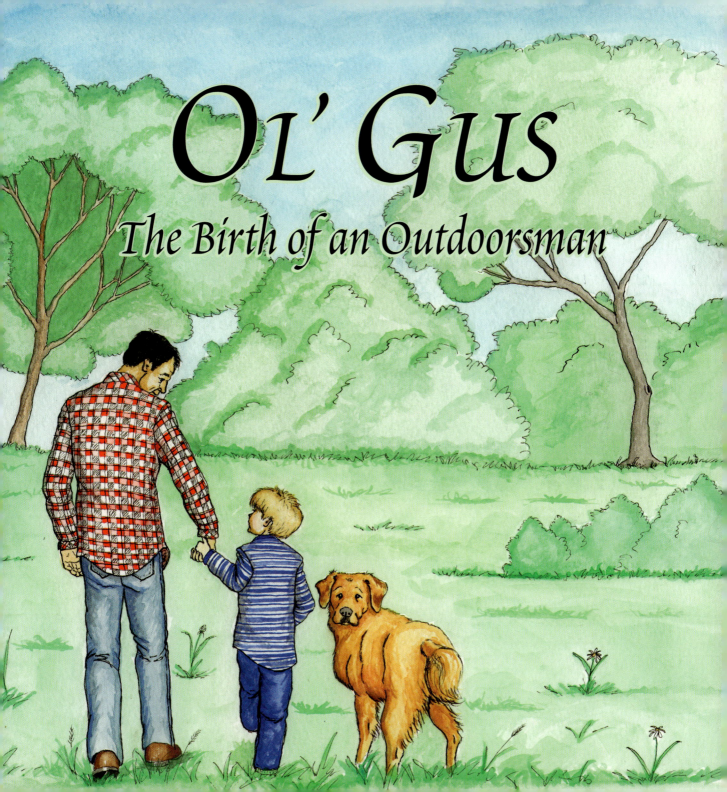

Dedication

This book is dedicated to my son Wyatt. For enriching my life for the last 22 years, for the wonderful memories at the baseball diamonds, the woods and fields, and on the lakes we've fished. You are my companion, my best friend and most of all, a great Son.

ISBN: 978-0-9842147-1-6

Text and Illustrations Copyright 2010 by Dudley King

Designed and Printed by Panacea Press - Murfreesboro, TN 37129
615-406-8222

All rights reserved, no part of this publication may be reproduced, transmitted in any form by any means, electronic, mechanical, photocopy, recording or otherwise, without written permission from the publisher, except as provided by USA copyright law.

OL' GUS

What do you want to do today Gus? The sun is just coming up, I bet there's something we can take care of outside, what do you think Gus? Whoa, did you hear that Gus? What was it? Gus, was it that saber tooth squirrel? No, we took care of him last week. Was it a buffalo, Gus? No, we took care of him too. Gus, was it stampeding elephants, was it more of those parent eating spiders, was it Martians, was it the boogyman, (No, even Gus knows there's no such thing as a boogyman), was it the bad guys, maybe it was a monster?

I know I heard something, didn't you Gus? There's something out there Gus! Be careful Gus, lets go take care of it!

I hope you and your child enjoy reading the adventures of Ol' Gus, my "BB Gun".

Because there's still a little bit of child in all of us.

THE BUMBLE BEES

Growing up in the city, there were always friends over to play baseball, football, riding bikes and all the fun things that kids do. But the weekends were special. My Grandparents had a farm about 45 minutes away and we went there most weekends. They had animals on the farm, a creek, and a farm house with a big front porch. On the front porch is where I was introduced to shooting.

I remember watching my Dad shoot varmits from 300 yards and I saw my Grandfather shoot a squirrel with his 22 rifle from 100 yards. But what impressed me most of all, was my Grandfather shooting Bumble Bees using a BB gun. There were always Bumble Bees buzzing around the flowers in front of the porch. I wondered how anyone could shoot a Bumble Bee in mid-air, but he could.

It wasn't very long before I got Gus. The farm brought on a new experience for me. My Dad and Grandfather taught me the safe way to handle a gun. "Always treat a gun as if it was loaded, make sure of your target and what's beyond it, and most of all, watch that muzzle," they said. I was also taught how to shoot. "Aim, take a deep breath, and slowly squeeze the trigger until the gun goes off." With a little practice, I was popping those bumble bees right out of the air!

THE MULBERRY TREE

A Mulberry Tree normally grows 30 to 40 feet tall with lots of branches and leaves. In the late spring, they produce Mulberries and most of all, birds LOVE them! Once the berries begin to ripen, the fun begins. All my friends had BB guns and on any particular day, we could count on three or four of us at the tree. The birds would flock to the tree. Sometimes there would be 15 to 20 birds scrambling limb to limb to get the berries. They loved the berries so much we would shoot at one and a minute later the flock would fly right back to the tree. Most of the birds were Starlings, a medium size black bird. They have a walk that reminded us of Ms. Pritchard, a lady that worked in the school cafeteria. She was a nice lady and she liked all of us. Ms. Pritchard was a LARGE lady, so large she had to swing her legs side to side instead of front to back. Unfortunately for us, she liked our lunch more than we did. We had to run to lunch everyday hoping that Ms. Prichard hadn't eaten all the good stuff! Well, back to the Mulberry Tree. We would spend days around the tree laughing about a bad shot and giving each other high fives after a good one! A couple of years later, we thought we had thinned out most of the Starlings. Wrong! There are still gazillions of them!

THE CHIMNEY SWIFTS

A Chimney Swift is a tiny bird that flies very fast and can turn on a dime. They dart around and can fly right into a chimney without even slowing down!

Me and Gus must have taken a million shots at the little jets and never got close except "one" time. We were hiding and waiting for an upcoming "Bogie." It was a single approaching fast from the south. We took aim leading the little jet by several yards and fired. I remember it like it was yesterday. It seemed like the BB and the Chimney Swift were in slow motion. The BB hit the jet and was falling with a large stream of smoke behind it and them, BOOM! CRASH AND BURN! It was an amazing shot!

Ol' Gus and me had taken down a "Russian Fighter Jet" and saved the country. We were National Heroes and ready for a ticker tape parade in our honor!

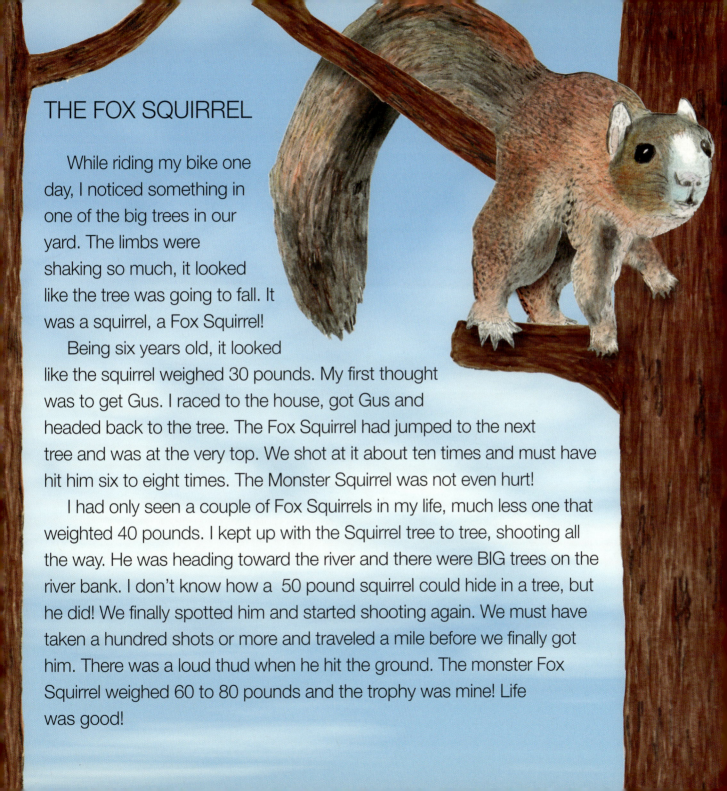

THE FOX SQUIRREL

    While riding my bike one day, I noticed something in one of the big trees in our yard. The limbs were shaking so much, it looked like the tree was going to fall. It was a squirrel, a Fox Squirrel!

    Being six years old, it looked like the squirrel weighed 30 pounds. My first thought was to get Gus. I raced to the house, got Gus and headed back to the tree. The Fox Squirrel had jumped to the next tree and was at the very top. We shot at it about ten times and must have hit him six to eight times. The Monster Squirrel was not even hurt!

    I had only seen a couple of Fox Squirrels in my life, much less one that weighted 40 pounds. I kept up with the Squirrel tree to tree, shooting all the way. He was heading toward the river and there were BIG trees on the river bank. I don't know how a 50 pound squirrel could hide in a tree, but he did! We finally spotted him and started shooting again. We must have taken a hundred shots or more and traveled a mile before we finally got him. There was a loud thud when he hit the ground. The monster Fox Squirrel weighed 60 to 80 pounds and the trophy was mine! Life was good!

THE DEACON

From the picnic table to the target on the back fence was about 50 yards. I've hit the bulls eye thousands of times from there with "Ol' Gus." I would imagine the target as anything from the "Joker or the Riddler" to the "Bad Guys". In reality it was just something to shoot at.

One day while shooting at the target, a bird landed on the fence right beside the target! I aimed and made a great shot. I jumped up and started to run toward the fence until I heard him. It was Mr. Dalton, a Deacon at our church. "That was a pretty good shot there but why did you have to shoot the little bird especially with a target right beside it," he asked? "That little bird is one of God's creatures," Mr. Dalton went on to say.

I was feeling pretty bad about that and Mr. Dalton could tell. He tried to cheer me up and asked about my BB gun. "I call him Gus, sir, I got him for my 6th birthday". "Well, it looks like he shoots pretty good, can I try?" "Sure Mr. Dalton." We were taking turns shooting at the target and I was doing a lot better than he was. This went on for a while and I think he was getting mad. It was my turn to shoot when another bird landed on the fence. I wanted to shoot the bird so bad, but before I could do anything, Mr. Dalton yanked Gus out of my hands and shot at the bird. Feathers went everywhere and the bird fell!

I looked at Mr. Dalton in amazement. He looked at me and said "what do you say we keep this just between me and you?" We never mentioned it again but walking into church every Sunday morning, Mr. Dalton would give me a little wink and a pat on my back!

THE DREAM

"Hurry guys, grab your BB guns, the Martians are coming, the Martians are coming!" Buster, Mark, Tim and me were out numbered, they're thousands of Flying Saucers on the horizon and they're getting closer. What are we going to do? Are we all going to die?

We heard several loud explosions, the Army had arrived but their missiles and bombs were bouncing off the UFO's.

The saucers were barely over the tree tops by now, we have to do something. Gus and I took a shot, the UFO exploded! We all started shooting at them, every one we hit, were completely destroyed! The UFO's could withstand missiles and bombs but they would not withstand Copper! Our copper BB's had saved the world!

"What a dream or was it?" There were thousands of BB sized holes in my ceiling and there was a scent of Martians in the air!

The moral of the story: If the Martians attack your neighborhood, don't call the Army, GRAB YOUR BB GUN!

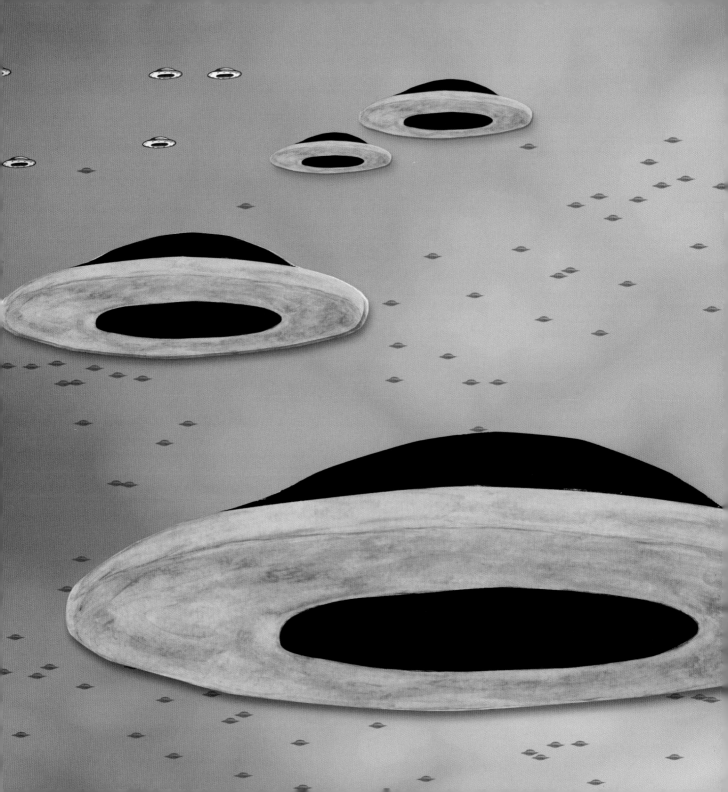

SPIDERS!

Most kids play some type of sport. If you play baseball, you fantasize that "this hit will win the Worlds Series" or if you play golf, "this putt is to win the Masters." I had those thoughts too, but growing up with Gus the stories were endless. Me and Gus saved my friends from the Killer Bumble Bees, we saved my parents from Dinosaurs and we even saved the world from Aliens.

But one day in the vacant lot, me and Gus walked upon the most horrifying thing of our lives, a huge Writing Spider! Everybody knows that if a spider writes your name in its web, you would die. This web read "Ms. Pritchar." The web needed only one letter and she would die! Me and Gus had "taken care" of a lot of things before, but this was life or death. We could not let that happen. We called the Police, "There's a huge Writing Spider here, hurry, Ms. Pritchard is about to die!" The SWAT team arrived in minutes and after a four hour battle, Ms. Pritchard was safe! The next day at school, Ms. Pritchard thanked me and gave me a double helping of beets!

THE TEST

Saturday morning was a ritual for me and Gus. Instead of watching cartoons or sleeping late, we were in the vacant lot at daylight "protecting the world" from any type of danger that may be lurking. One morning before we went outside, we heard a sound. Was it a turkey? We had never seen a turkey at our house, so me and Gus had to check it out. Without making a sound, we headed to the lot. We had two more steps to make around the bushes and we should be able to see where the sound was coming from.

There were two turkeys, a hen and a Monster Gobbler! The gobbler must have been six feet tall and his tail feathers flared out to eight feet wide! They were about 100 yards away, we had to get closer. We crawled across the lot, until we were 20 yards from the turkeys. The gobbler would turn side to side and the hen never moved. We watched them for 15 to 20 minutes, it was awesome! We heard something from the bushes, a Game Warden stepped out! He walked toward me and asked "why didn't you shoot the gobbler? I've been watching you the whole time." The warden scared me at first, but he shook my hand and again asked, "why didn't you shoot the turkey?" "Well sir, I was plenty close, me and Ol' Gus could have got him, but I didn't know if it was turkey season and anyways, I don't have a license." "Son, I'm proud of you. I want to give you my Hen decoy, it might help you take your first turkey one day. I thanked the warden, "Mr. Williams" for the decoy.
"You're very welcome," he said, "and by the way, call me Sam." We were friends for years!

THE TAXIDERMIST

Sharing photos with others is part of hunting and fishing. They preserve the memories for a lifetime. If you harvest an especially nice trophy, you can always have the animal preserved by a taxidermist.

   At age 10, I thought it would be cool to learn the art of taxidermy. There was a class you could purchase by mail and after a couple of weeks of studying, I was ready to go. My first animal was a duck, it turned out OK. The second try had to be perfect. Me and Gus took a gray squirrel one Saturday and after church the following day, I worked all afternoon and evening on the squirrel. To keep the hide soft, I wrapped it up in a damp towel and would finish it up after school the next day. All day long during school, my thoughts were on the squirrel. Finally school was over, a quick ride home and I would finish my perfect job as a taxidermist! I went to the garage, the towel was gone? Maybe my Dad had noticed that it was drying out and hoped he added a little water to the towel. He hadn't seen it? I looked everywhere. Finally, I asked my Mom if she had seen it. The look on her face was priceless, she had just put the last load of laundry in the dryer and the towel was in that load! The dryer was still running when we got there, I opened the door and fur went everywhere! My career as a taxidermist was over. Its funny thinking about it now, "I'm just glad my second try wasn't a Moose!"

HUBERT, HERSHEL AND HENRY

Drawing a deer tag to hunt Land Between the Lakes offered a great chance of bagging a really big Whitetail. The management area in Middle Tennessee was known to produce a lot of big bucks.

After scouting most of the area the day before the hunt, I found nothing promising and headed to camp for the evening. Driving back through the main road in LBL, I happened to notice a huge rub, one hundred yards away in deep woods.

I climbed the ridge and found that every big tree on that ridge and the next two ridges were rubbed raw. I hung my stand on the middle ridge giving me a great view of all three and then left the area.

The night before the hunt was a short one. Just wondering what the buck looked like kept me up all night, so I headed to the woods and was in my stand 2 hours before daylight.

At 7:30 that morning I noticed movement on the first ridge, it was a deer. I found the deer in my scope, it was a monster buck! I took the shot from 175 yard and he fell in his tracks! Walking up on the huge 10 pointer is a feeling that every hunter should experience at least once in their life. He was the biggest buck I'd ever seen, dead or alive.

The buck, "Hubert", hangs on the wall next to "Hershel and Henry", both are big 9 pointers. Even though its been more than 25 years since taking Hubert, he still reminds me of the excitement of that special morning.

THE PAST, THE PRESENT AND THE FUTURE

Life was different back in the late 60s and early 70s than what it is today. It was common to see a gun rack mounted in the back window of a truck holding rifles or shotguns. There was never a problem finding a place to hunt, things have definitely changed.

On Thanksgiving morning, my Dad, Grandfather, and Uncles would go rabbit hunting while my Mother, Grandmother, and Aunts cooked the afternoon meal. They laughed and enjoyed each other's company. The dinner was always wonderful. It was one of the few meals we (the kids) could fill our plates with what we wanted to eat instead of what was good for us.

On Sunday evenings, we looked forward to watching a couple of outdoor television shows; *The American Sportsman,* with host Curt Gowdy, and then *Mutual of Omaha's Wild Kingdom*, with Marlin Perkins and his co-host Jim Fowler. Those were the good old days.

My grandparents passed away years ago. The kids are grown now and have kids of their own. We all get together every year or two and its always nice, but its not the way it was as a child.

I'm 53 years old now and lived nineteen years longer than the doctors said I would due to Cancer. My son was three years old when I was told I had six months to live. I was going to miss all the special things that all parents look forward to. Today, my son Wyatt, is a senior in college. We look at old photos and tell stories of his first BB gun, his first fish, first squirrel, deer, and the list goes on and on. These are things I never thought I would experience. Today, it doesn't matter who bags the biggest deer or catches the most fish, it's just spending time together in the outdoors.

Years ago, when I thought my life may be short, I began to see things differently. A sunrise or sunset seemed much more spectacular. Watching a storm approaching from a distance was relaxing. Strangely enough, I began to hear a different sound of silence, one that was much more peaceful. The "little things" didn't seem so little anymore.

The Lord has definitely watched over me and my family. One of the biggest thrills of my life has yet to come, the day my Son has a family of his own, and wants his Dad to help him with his son or daughter's first BB gun!

The 10 Commandments for Gun Safety

1. Treat every gun with the respect due a loaded gun.
   This is the cardinal rule of gun safety.

2. Always be aware of where the muzzle of the gun is pointing.

3. Unload guns when not in use.

4. Always be sure that the barrel is clear of obstructions.

5. Be sure of your target and what's beyond it.

6. Never point a gun at anything you do not intend to shoot.

7. Never climb a tree or fence or jump a ditch with a loaded firearm.

8. Never shoot at a flat hard surface or the surface of water.

9. Store guns and ammunition separately.

10. Do not mix firearms and alcohol.

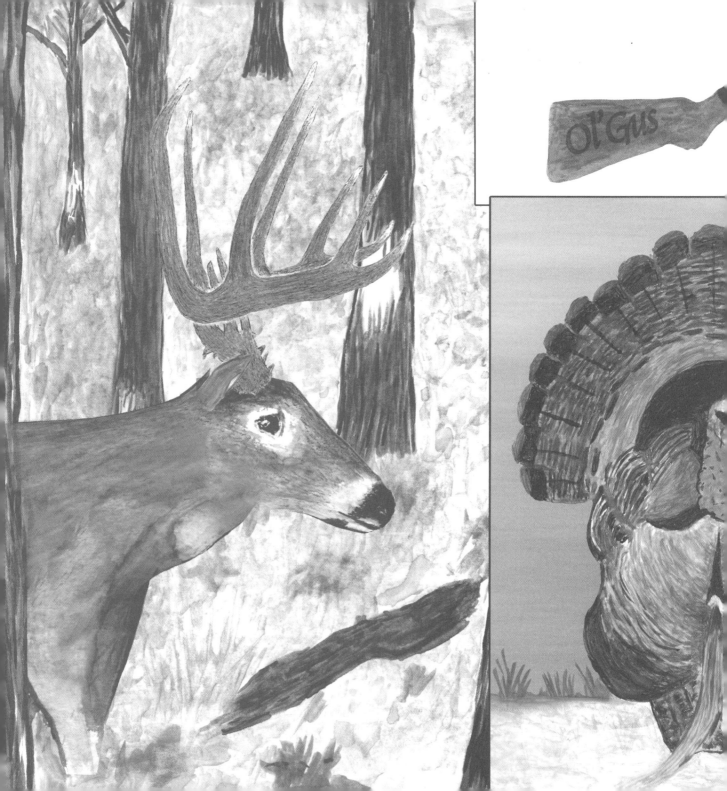